START STRONG

Advice for Young Pastors

DR. WALTER C. JACKSON

WESTBOW
PRESS®
A DIVISION OF THOMAS NELSON
& ZONDERVAN

WestBow Press books may be ordered through booksellers or by contacting:

WestBow Press
A Division of Thomas Nelson & Zondervan
1663 Liberty Drive
Bloomington, IN 47403
www.westbowpress.com
1 (866) 928-1240

ISBN: 978-1-5127-6097-2 (sc)
ISBN: 978-1-5127-6098-9 (e)

Library of Congress Control Number: 2016917277

Print information available on the last page.

WestBow Press rev. date: 10/27/2016

Brother Billy Crosby, Pastor Emeritus Summer Grove Baptist Church, Shreveport, Louisiana

Young Pastor, the book you are about to read deals with the basic fundamentals of a pastor who desires to be pleasing to God. My "son in the ministry," Walter Jackson, has poured out his heart for all to profit by his mistakes and successes. As his pastor, I can truthfully say from the beginning of his ministry he was *all in*! His commitment to be the best pastor, preacher, husband, father, friend, and community leader are second to none! I appreciate his openness and honesty that makes these chapters so real. A famous football coach of the Green Bay Packers won the Super Bowl by teaching his players the basic fundamentals of the game of football. Walter has the same message to all who aspire to be called pastor! So, young men, preach the Word, love your people (where they are), don't be lazy, don't be a mooch, and let God's will be your primary agenda! And beloved, every church you pastor will be sad when you are called to another field. PS: Every October during Pastor Appreciation Month for several years Walter has written me a note of *thanks* for the contribution God allowed me to make in his life! Years ago after preaching a revival for me, I received this note from the evangelist: "Thanksgiving is the vibration of the soul's heartstrings under the soft touch of God's benevolence" Then he added these words: "Perhaps the easiest, yet least practiced of all Christian virtues is the fine art of being grateful for one's blessing!" Therefore, at least once a year, Pastor, take your heart out of cold storage, and bless someone who has made an impact on your life! I believe the Bible is ... (Heb. 4:12). *Well, glory!*

Pastor Michael Waters, Senior Pastor Parkwood Baptist Church, Concord, North Carolina

A pastor needs many tools in his toolbox for ministry, and wise counsel is certainly one he cannot do without. Proverbs 11:14 says, "For lack of guidance a nation falls, but victory is won through many advisers" (NIV). The same verse in the ESV reads, "But in an abundance of counselors there is safety." Having been a senior pastor for over twenty-two years, I can honestly say being a pastor is not "safe," but it is rewarding! In the dangerous places I have benefited from wise counsel. Over the years, there have been times when a wise word from another pastor has helped me not only keep my sanity but protected the ministry in which I have served. Walter Jackson's book *Start Strong* comes from fire-tested experience and a heart for God's shepherds. In this book to pastors, Walter speaks the truth in love and has a heart to see God's leaders succeed in ministry. There are many tools that are important for ministry, but some are essential. If you are starting your ministry or need to be sharpened, the advice contained here is essential to your toolbox.

Dr. Steve Hunter, Hope for the Heart Chair of Biblical Counseling, Criswell College, Dallas, Texas

It is important for all of us to soak in wisdom from those who practice what they preach and who have remained faithful through the test of time. That is Dr. Walter Jackson. It has been my privilege to know him for over thirty years—as a mentor, and more importantly, as a friend. I sure wish I had this little book when I began as a pastor. It would have saved me a lot of grief and regret along the way. Reading Walter's words was a great encouragement and inspiration to me after twenty-five years in the ministry. I know Walter's words of wisdom will be a tremendous blessing for you as well—no matter how long you have been in ministry. Thanks for sharing your life and your heart, my friend.

Dr. Earl Waggoner, Dean, Biblical Studies and Theology; Colorado Christian University

Dr. Jackson has crafted an engaging, concise, and highly accessible book. His six chapters provide wonderfully practical and godly advice for any pastor, especially one just beginning the work. What I found most appealing were all the stories shared by the author. He's obviously lived what he's sharing, a fact that adds depth and great value to his words. I am so happy to commend this book.

Contents

Acknowledgments

I am so grateful to the following people who gave of themselves to help me put this project together.

Brother Billy Crosby: The Lord called me to the ministry under the ministry of Brother Billy. It is his preaching that developed in me a love for the Bible and understanding it to be the inerrant word of God. I learned more about preaching from Brother Billy than from anyone else and still today occasionally while preaching I will think, *That really sounded like something Brother Billy would say.* I still consider it a blessing to call him my pastor, and I forever will.

Dr. Earl Waggoner: Earl and I first met in the youth group at Northwest Memorial. Though we went to different high schools, we became friends and enjoyed a summer working together hanging sheetrock in a downtown Houston high rise. We shared some great times that summer. I have so many memories of laughter we enjoyed as Earl is one of the funniest people I have ever known. He has been a pastor, taught at Golden Gate Seminary (now Gateway Seminary), and is now dean at CCU. I am grateful for his friendship and advice he gave me as I was pursuing my DMin.

Dr. Steve Hunter: Steve and I met at Southwestern Seminary. Though we attended the same high school, he was a sophomore when I was a senior. We became good friends, and as you will read, he was used of the Lord in my being called to Seventh and Main Baptist Church in Bonham. He has been such an encourager to me through the years, and I have appreciated his help in ministry on many occasions. Steve has been a pastor, international missionary, counselor, and college and seminary professor.

Gary Chaffin: One of the smartest and funniest people I know! Gary is a member at First Baptist in DeKalb and remains a good friend though the miles now separate us. His feedback on this little project was so encouraging and helpful. Hopefully this book reads smoother because of him. I am grateful to the Lord for allowing our paths to cross and even more so to call him my friend.

Dr. Robert Webb, a.k.a., Pastor Awesome: Robert and I met at Houston Baptist University. He reminded me some years after he and his sweet wife, Debbie, were married that I was the one who introduced them. It is a wonderful thing to have someone so smart and well connected that I can hold that over him for favors such as his advice on this book. Great advice, by the way, that helped me think ahead through the project. He is senior pastor at Calvary Baptist Church in Kaufman, Texas.

Pastor Michael Waters: Michael and I met when we pastored in the Bonham area. He is one of those men I cherished spending Monday afternoons praying with. He is senior pastor at Parkwood Baptist Church in Concord, North Carolina, and has been there since November of 2009.

Dr. Rebecca Dowden: We have known each other since high school as we both were in the youth group at Northwest Memorial Baptist Church. Dr. Dowden edited this project for me and also did the editing on my doctoral project! She is currently a professor at the University of St. Thomas, teaching business communication and a research and writing class in the MBA program.

Landon, Logan, and Lauren: Our kids—you put up with a lot, you missed out on some things, and you were blessed to enjoy some things. I pray that you realize the older you get how good God has been to you and to us as a family. Thank you for encouraging me through the years.

My wife, Lisa: Without her faithful, loving support, I would not have lasted in the ministry. My biggest supporter and defender as well as when needed, loving critic. Her generosity never ceases to amaze me, and her encouragement keeps me going. Thank you, dear. I love you.

And as I hope is obvious, glory to God for His love, patience, compassion, and unending help not only to me but to everyone He calls into service for His kingdom. I thank Him for the privilege to know Him and to be used by Him in His ministry to reach the world one life at a time.

Introduction

Why another little book on pastoring? It's not really because I think I have something to say that everyone should hear or that my advice is going to be better than any you've heard or read before. Not because there needs to be another theological treatise on pastoring. In fact, this little project is written from the heart based on real-life experience. It's not about theology or doctrine. It's not another philosophy of ministry book. It is fairly simple and I believe highly practical.

So, why another book? Let me explain it this way.

When I was a teenager and then college and seminary age, things were much different from the way they are now, but two things in particular. One, if you were the person who made friends with the teacher or professor, you were seen as trying to butter them up in order to get some advantage over everyone else. Back in that day and time you were not seen by others as very cool. Today, however, that is known as "networking" and is a very good thing to do. I missed out there, desiring more to be thought of as cool. The second thing was that I had no idea about getting started in ministry and the idea of looking for a mentor. I didn't know that I should have gone to my pastor during college and especially seminary and asked if I could spend time with him, shadow him, go on visits with him, just learn from him. This was another opportunity for learning that I missed out on.

The purpose, then, of this book, the reason for writing it, is that I determined if I ever had the opportunity to help a young pastor, I would take it. And so this advice comes with that intention and desire—to help you *Start Strong*. What I missed out on, I want to make sure others don't miss. My prayer is that this bit of information, experiential advice, firsthand observation, and learning will help you as you begin your ministry. And this is not just advice that will help the new pastor. Any area of ministry you are in and just starting out or still very early in the journey, this will benefit you also. So even if you are not a pastor, I hope you will read this little book and take it to heart. These six things served me very well during my pastoral ministry. I believe they will help you too. So the reason for writing it is that I want you to *Start Strong*, so let me begin ...

It was a summer day in 1980. I had recently graduated from high school in Northwest Houston and was working a summer job for a sheet metal company. My dream for years had been to play college and professional baseball. Our senior year, we, the varsity baseball team of Cypress Creek High School, made it to the Texas State Tournament at Disch-Falk Field on the University of Texas campus in Austin. We were in the final four of the big high schools in the state. We lost our semifinal game and so were out of the tournament. I like to tell people we were the third-best team in the state, because we played in the second game that first evening. In my mind the team that lost in the first game was fourth, making us third. Don't really think that's official, but it sounds good.

I didn't really have a plan B if the baseball career didn't work out, but since I wasn't a great player, I wasn't looked at by any colleges. After all I was about five foot six inches tall and weighed 120 pounds soaking wet, was not very quick, and had an average arm playing second base. Well, I registered to go to Sam Houston

State University in Huntsville, Texas, because that is where our coach had played, and they had a great program. I planned to try out as a walk on.

That all changed one day while working for the sheet metal company. We were making the air-conditioning ducts for a new Shell Oil office complex being built on I-10 just west of downtown Houston. Another summer worker and I were delivering the duct work. Now, I grew up around construction workers—my dad was a custom home builder and architect—so the atmosphere and even the language weren't anything new to me. But something this particular summer day was a bit different.

We were on the second floor of a building. It was simply the concrete structure at the time, no walls, just open air. A crane had lifted the box off of our truck up to the second floor, and there were about five or six on site workers helping us unload. As I mentioned, the construction site language wasn't really new to me. I did think it odd that there was a woman on the construction site. Remember this was 1980, and a woman construction worker wasn't typical. I just felt a bit out of place this day, listening to the conversations about who was going where after work and where they had been last night.

As we finished and were walking away, I will never forget the experience. It is as though the Lord played out an image in my mind that was as clear as if it were happening right before me. I imagined one of these guys arriving home late after work, late because he had stopped off at the local bar to drink away part of the family paycheck. As he came through the front door, his two little kids ran to greet him and jump in his arms. He smelled of cigarettes and beer. And then the Lord spoke to me louder in my heart than any voice I have ever heard: "Walter, I want you to tell people there is a better way to live." So here I am, just graduated from high school preparing to go off to my first semester of college, walking down the stairs at this construction site, and I'm crying. That was the moment I knew the Lord was calling me to ministry.

I had been very involved in our church youth group, one of the leaders. Beginning our junior year of high school, I was one of the founding members of a Christian organization, Cougars for Christ, and was the first president.

But this was bigger than all that. Full-time Christian ministry. In an instant the desire to play baseball was gone, and I knew I probably wouldn't complete my college education at Sam Houston State. After one semester at Sam, I transferred to Houston Baptist University, where I received my bachelor of arts with a double major in Christianity and psychology. From there it was on to Southwestern Baptist Theological Seminary in Fort Worth, Texas. I earned a master of divinity and was ready to serve in a church. All I really knew back in that day was that you would be a youth minister, and when the kids could outrun you, you became a pastor. So that was my plan. After a very difficult first position as a youth minister, I quit after seven months (too long of a difficult story to tell here). My wife, our young son, Landon, and I moved back to Houston and temporarily in with my parents.

I began working—yep, construction—for a good friend I had gone to church with while I was a teenager and through college. God has a wonderful way of connecting us for His glory and His plan. My uncle Bobby worked at Cameron Iron works. One day while talking with another man at work, Floyd, the conversation about church came up. Floyd was a member of the First Baptist Church in Magnolia, Texas. He mentioned they had started a mission church a few years before and that little church was looking for a pastor. Uncle Bobby told him about me, and within a few months I was pastoring my first church, Silver

Springs Baptist Church, still officially a mission of First Baptist at the time.

I'll just say that experience was quite a learning one. Some really good things took place and some pretty difficult ones; so goes the ministry. I was there as a bi-vocational pastor for a year and eight months, still doing construction and building custom furniture. It didn't end well. Because the church was a mission of First Baptist, Dr. Ed Seay, who is a wonderful pastor, moved me over to First Baptist as his associate. I will be forever grateful to him and to First Baptist for their help and encouragement. I learned a great deal about being a pastor from watching and listening to Dr. Ed.

In August of 1993, a dear friend who was pastoring a church in North Texas invited me up to preach a revival, Dr. Steve Hunter, who is now on the faculty at Criswell College in Dallas. Steve told me before I came that there were several churches in the area who were looking for a pastor, and he wanted to send them my resume and tell them I would be preaching the revival. One of the pastor search committees from a church came each night to the revival and on the last night asked to visit with me. It was an exciting time with Seventh and Main Baptist Church in Bonham, Texas. To shorten the story and get to the heart of this book, I'll just fill in the important note. I became the pastor of Seventh and Main in October of 1993. It was my first full-time church.

It was while pastoring Seventh and Main that some of the best advice I was ever given came to me. The advice makes up the first two chapters of this book.

Chapter 1

PREACH THE WORD

I often think of myself as being very organized; it's a self-deception. I think I am pretty good at making notes of important events. But the problem is that after some time, I cannot remember where I recorded those important notes. Or when I do find them, they lack details I thought I had included. Such is the case regarding the two events that offer the first two words of advice I want to pass along. I read through the journal that I kept while I was the pastor of Seventh and Main and was able to find where I recorded one of the two moments. It was on Thursday, October 13, 1994.

During my first couple of years at Seventh and Main, two different couples brought by the church an older, retired pastor they wanted me to meet. I love this because these two couples, who were both members of the church, had no idea the other couple had done what they did. It happened twice with two different retired pastors. These pastors were friends with these couples, and they wanted me to meet their pastor-friends.

I was grateful for the visit. I asked each of these men the same question. I considered myself a young pastor—I was thirty-two at the time—and there were a few people in the church who really thought I was not just young but, "young and needed lots of training." That's church member code for needing to learn to do things their way when they want. But that's another topic. So I asked each of these pastors, "What advice would you give me as a young pastor?" Remember, this took place between these two men on different occasions, and the men didn't know each other. They both gave me the same advice: "Preach the Word, and love the people."

I want to add a note about my ministry at this point. I pastored bivocationally as an associate and then in three full-time pastorates from 1991 until 2012. I know pastors who have served in one church longer than that. So I realize I am not as much a veteran of pastoral ministry as many are. I began in the ministry as an associational director of missions in June of 2012. Also, the largest church I pastored was the last one, the First Baptist Church of DeKalb, Texas, where I served for eleven years. A good estimate on our worship attendance for that time was 285. I know I could say ministerially speaking, we averaged 300, but 285 is a pretty accurate across the board average. The highest attendance day we had was my first Easter in DeKalb. We did count that day and had 405 in worship. I share that bit of information to let you know I have never served a megachurch. In fact, I can say that of the four churches I served, the average attendances while I was there were 35, 85, 135, and 285. I guess I wanted to add this for those of you serving or who will serve in what statistics tell us are small to average churches.

It is at this point I would love to include a sermon I preached in February 2016 from Nehemiah to encourage you that your work for the Lord is important, regardless of how you or others may see it. Chances are you will serve during your ministry life in a church that averages fewer than three hundred. That's just the way it is. And trust me, that's okay. In fact, it is wonderful.

So, of the six bits of advice I want to offer you, the first two came from these conversations. The first one is this: "Preach the Word."

As I write this, it is March/April 2016, and I am fifty-four years old. The church in general is in a state of flux. Every day it seems there are articles, books, blogs, and podcasts coming out about how the church needs to change and be this or that. The latest megachurch or most popular parachurch pastors tell us what works to reach the current generation. I believe the advice I am passing on to you fits whatever genre of church you serve in or want to start, and time does not change these realities. I'm not going to propose a new church idea; these are things that are people-oriented. Did you know that most pastors who are fired or forced out are so not over theological issues but rather, relationship issues? It's true. And in many cases, the termination comes at the hands of ten or fewer people.[1]

According to an article in *Baptist Press* with Dr. Hershael York, a preaching professor at Southern Baptist Theological Seminary and pastor at Buck Run Baptist Church in Frankfort, Kentucky,

Between 23 and 41 percent of pastors experience "forced termination" at least once, according to an article published last year in the *Journal of Religion and Health*. Some 452 Southern Baptist pastors and staff members were forcibly terminated in 2012, according to a forced termination report compiled by state Baptist convention workers who deal with church conflict. The most common causes of forced termination among Southern Baptists are "control issues," "pastor's leadership style" and "poor people skills on the part of the pastor," according to the forced termination report. Among the top 15 causes of forced terminations, only two are related

---

[1] *The Baptist Courier*, https://baptistcourier.com/2013/01/pastoral-termination-an-epidemic/.

to sin by the pastor—"ethical misconduct" at number 8 and "sexual misconduct" at number 10.[2]

I'm including in the footnotes at this point the web address for two more articles[3] that address this situation. I do so hoping to help you understand the importance of being relational in your ministry. This will be addressed in the chapters to come, but I add it here because it is essential to know there is more to pastoring than what you do and say in the pulpit.

I was not an awesome pastor, evidenced by the reality that before picking up this book you probably never heard of me. But I do believe I was effective at least in part—no, to a great extent—because I understood these six things and made certain they were how I went about my ministry.

"Preach the Word." Well, where do you go with this one in a day and age where any number of things are set forth about how you should preach in the local church today? I will forever be grateful for the pastor who to this day I call "my pastor." I thank God for putting me in Northwest Memorial Baptist Church, now Houston Northwest Baptist Church. Brother Billy Crosby came to be our pastor, and my life was forever changed. I developed a love for the Bible through the preaching ministry of Brother Billy. He has since retired but still preaches regularly.

Another personal side story. One Sunday morning in DeKalb, I was standing at the back of the church, which faced our parking lot, greeting people as they arrived. A woman who I almost recognized walked through the door. I introduced myself and

---

[2] *Baptist Press,* http://www.bpnews.net/43286/
pastoral-termination-common-but-often-avoidable-experts-say.

[3] Thom Rainer blog, http://thomrainer.com/2016/01/six-things-you-need-to-know-about-pastors-who-leave-their-ministry/;Lifeway Study. http://lifewayresearch.com/2016/01/12/former-pastors-report-lack-of-support-led-to-abandoning-pastorate/.

asked her name. She responded, "Well, you should know me." Then I saw the man standing behind her. It was Mrs. Annette and Brother Billy! In my defense, she wasn't wearing glasses, and I seemed to remember that she used to. But wow! Brother Billy was at our church. He had been doing interim work in Shreveport, Louisiana and had his first day off of preaching in a number of months. He said he wanted to come see one of his "preacher boys." I was thrilled and terrified at the same time. It was one of those Sundays. For one thing, our minister of music was out that day. No matter who you have filling in, it's just not the same, and the service never goes as smoothly. Add to that we were having trouble with our projector, and hanging from the ceiling above the pulpit was a pipe with wires sticking out of it. Plus, we had been having trouble with the air-conditioning, and it was a bit warm in the sanctuary. And it just wasn't one of my better sermons. Of all the days to have my hero in the faith show up for a service.

Brother Billy Crosby preaches the Word. In fact, he starts every sermon with this statement, which I memorized back in high school from hearing him declare it every Sunday morning:

I believe the Bible is the Word of God, and in this book we find these words, Hebrews 4:12: "For the Word of God is quick and powerful and sharper than any two-edged sword, piercing even to the dividing asunder of soul and spirit and of the joints and marrow, and is a discerner of the thoughts and intents of the heart." In Romans 10:17, the Bible says, "So then faith cometh by hearing and hearing by the Word of God." And I contend that if faith cometh by hearing and hearing by the Word of God, then faith for those who are lost to be saved comes by hearing the Word of God. And faith for those who are already saved to grow up into spiritual maturity also comes by hearing the Word of God. Now take your Bibles if you will and turn to …

5

Every Sunday Brother Billy preached the Word. To this day, my greatest influence in preaching has not been the preaching class I had at Houston Baptist University or the classes at Southwestern or from the books I read and papers I wrote while pursuing my doctorate. It was from the Sunday morning and Sunday night preaching of Brother Billy Crosby.

He believed the Bible to be the inerrant, infallible Word of God and he preached it as such. And it formed me to a great extent into the preacher I became and still am. He didn't apologize for any of it, he didn't skirt around any of it, he read it, expounded upon it, applied it, and declared it, and then also, he lived it, and still does. I have had the great joy of having Brother Billy in two of the churches I pastored. He preached a revival for me in Texarkana, and he came and preached at my tenth anniversary in DeKalb. I still have an old cassette tape holder and in it are a number of his sermons from the 1980s.

I made it a habit of preaching expository sermons while I pastored. I personally believe that is the best preaching. It takes your people through large sections of scripture and even entire books of the Bible. It helps them see the big picture of scripture in context, and it also keeps you from dodging issues, if it's in the text you preach it.

One of the pastors I asked to proof this project suggested I explain or define expository preaching. And since it is best not to assume things, though perhaps you remember this from a preaching class, let's review.

In a Lifeway article, Wayne McDill states it this way:

The word exposition is from the Latin, *exposito*, meaning "a setting forth, narration, or display." As applied to preaching, the word has come to mean the setting forth or explanation of the message of the biblical text. In expository preaching the sermon is designed to communicate what the text says, including its meaning for the contemporary audience.[4]

In a wonderful book "Preaching to a Shifting Culture" Haddon Robinson writes:

In the broadest sense, it is preaching that draws its substance from the Scriptures. It is to ask, "When I approach the Scriptures for a message to preach do I allow the Bible to shape my sermon, or do I let what I have already decided to say determine what I take from the Bible?"[5]

As you do this, it is amazing how the Lord will bring you to a passage of scripture in a timely moment for your church or even just for some specific people. I remember one time while in Bonham, I was in the bank making a deposit. One of our members worked there. She pulled me aside and asked if she could ask me a question. Of course, she then asked how long I had been standing outside their Sunday school classroom. I was just a bit confused. She told me that over the past several weeks, conversations that had come up in their class were the precise thing I preached about in the morning service! I told her I was simply preaching through wherever we were at the time and that the Lord was working to speak to their hearts. Amazing how many times something similar to that has happened through the years.

Another advantage to preaching expository sermons through the Bible is it helps greatly with your sermon preparation. I have always told people that I operate by what I call "structured flexibility." That is, I would have a plan for each day, but it could be interrupted at any time. And when you are preaching through

---

[4] Lifeway, http://lifeway.com/2014/01/08/ seven-qualities-of-expository-preaching/

[5] Haddon W. Robinson, *Preaching to a Shifting Culture* (Grand Rapids, MI: Baker Books, 2004), 82.

books of the Bible, even when interrupted, you know right where you are when you get back to the study.

Yes, I would from time to time do a topical series, but not very often. Yes, I would interrupt a series for the holidays, or a special occasion, or even if a tragedy occurred that I felt needed to be addressed. But by and large, I stuck to the practice of expository preaching. And so on my shelves now I have twenty-three—yes, twenty-three—three-ring binders of sermon manuscripts of partial or complete verse-by-verse sermons through books of the Bible. I don't say that to brag, just to emphasize what I believe is the best way to preach. Another advantage to this over time is that now when I am going back to a passage of scripture to preach, chances are I already have a good deal of study material I can draw from.

It may have caught your eye that I mentioned I have notebooks of "manuscripts." I was taught in school that you begin with an outline, write a manuscript, and then develop a detailed outline that you take to the pulpit. I could just never get there. One reason was if I thought of something while studying on Tuesday, if I did not write it out in detail, it was a guarantee I would forget it by Sunday. So I got in the habit of writing and preaching from a manuscript. I would review it until I had it pictured enough in my mind that I did not have to read it on Sunday morning. I didn't memorize it, but I did picturize it. In other words, I knew where to look on the page when I needed to look. Having a manuscript also kept me focused. It is a dangerous thing when I would get off the page because an idea popped into my head and I decided to chase it. For me, those didn't always turn out well, especially when I would have a thought and begin to go with it and then forget what the point was going to be. It made for a good laugh with the congregation but frustrating that I thought I had a good point to make and couldn't remember it. That's just me—I am most comfortable with a manuscript before me.

Regardless of your method of taking material to the pulpit, preach the Word. Another important element in preaching is that I firmly believe eye contact with your congregation is essential. Don't read your sermon, don't stare at the notes, and don't stare at the ground; look at your folks. I have been amazed over the years of sitting in services where the preacher never looked at anybody. I tried to make eye contact with every person in the church during the course of the sermon. Connect with people, looking them in the eyes, and you can also see when and who the Holy Spirit is dealing with during the service. So, I preferred manuscripts, not with every sermon I preached but with the majority. I made an effort to look every person in the eyes during the sermon. Find the method that works for you and preach, but as you preach, preach the Word.

I will add here that I am a teacher at heart. Every spiritual gifts inventory I ever took confirmed that. I considered myself a teaching preacher in that I didn't always have a cute or funny opening story, I didn't always have a great illustration with every point, and I most certainly did not have a poem to end the message with. Nothing wrong with those things, but if they take up time in which you could be explaining scripture, then I would prefer scripture. I remember hearing a tremendous point, and I would give credit to whom credit is due, but I do not remember who said it. If a story you are telling overpowers the scripture you are preaching, don't tell the story. In other words, if people are going to remember the story more than the scripture, you lose and they lose, and especially if it is one of those emotional stories that doesn't have a good ending or a clear ending. That is what the congregation will remember.

The Word of God is what changes lives, so preach the Word!

I would also say—and this is something you will read in every book on preaching—never, never go to the pulpit unprepared. Be convicted by the words of 2 Timothy 2:15, "Be diligent to present yourself approved to God as a workman who does not need to be ashamed, accurately handling the word of truth." Paul went on to write to the young preacher Timothy in 4:1–2, "I solemnly charge you in the presence of God and of Christ Jesus, who is to judge the living and the dead, and by His appearing and His kingdom: preach the word; be ready in season and out of season; reprove, rebuke, exhort, with great patience and instruction." I trust you are familiar with the next three verses. Young preacher, you are living in the reality of those next three verses, which make verses 1 and 2 that much more important.

Distractions are going to come, emergencies are going to happen, and you will be drawn away from your study. Be sure you get back to your study, even if it means losing sleep. I remember running into another pastor on a Wednesday afternoon. He began to tell me that his folks were just going to have to understand that he didn't have a Bible study prepared for the night's service. He said that he had spent most of the day at the hospital with a family as a member of the family was having surgery, so he just didn't have time to prepare. I didn't say anything to the young man, who was about ten years younger than I was, but my thoughts were, *What about Monday and Tuesday? What were you doing then?* There are going to be extreme emergencies that come up, but I can tell you that in more than twenty years of being a pastor, I never once had an occasion that kept me from being able to prepare for a Sunday or Wednesday. They can happen, but I believe they are rare. This is another case I would make for the benefit of expository preaching. No matter the distractions, if you finished up chapter 2 in your last sermon, you know you are preparing to preach chapter 3, the first few verses at least. You are not scrambling for a topic; you are studying the text and preparing to explain it and apply it to life for your folks.

Whatever style you prefer, whatever method you use, when and as you preach—preach the Word!

LOVE THE PEOPLE

The second thing that I pass along to you was the second part of what each of these elderly pastors shared with me, "Love the people."

I will never forget the greatest compliment I was ever given. It happened in a funeral home; I know that sounds strange. One of our church members had died, and it was the evening before the memorial service, the visitation time for people to come and view the body and share their condolences with the family. There was a large crowd that evening, and I had already been in the chapel area to visit with the family. I was out in the lobby still talking with folks. John Ed and Reva Hutchinson came in. They were not at the time members of our church. Their son and his family were, and they joined sometime after. I was saying hello to them and talking briefly when Mrs. Reva said, "You know, Brother Walter, you are not just a great preacher but you are also a wonderful pastor. And you know there is a difference in the two." That meant so much to me because it is what I wanted to be. It is what I worked at being. And those were honestly her words.

Young pastor, love your people. I remember years ago hearing the important message, "People will put up with average preaching for good pastoring. But the greatest preaching w not make up for poor pastoring." That is a good word for you to hang on to.

It really doesn't matter the context of where you will be serving, country or suburbs, small community or big city, small rural church or mega church, people need to know they are loved. H. B. London Jr. of Focus on the Family wrote to ministers in his book *The Heart of a Great Pastor*, "Bloom where you are planted."[6] In the church God allows you to serve, love the people, and that means spending time among them. One way this is accomplished is by visiting them in their homes. When I pastored in Magnolia at Silver Springs, there were four neighborhoods around this little country church. In three of them there was never a hesitation to walk up to any home and knock on the door and be greeted. The other area, though, a couple of miles down the county road from the church, not so much. I will never forget one day I was out knocking on doors. Keep in mind this was in the country, the thick piney woods of Southeast Texas.

No one answered, so I turned to walk the sidewalk back to my car when an older man appeared beside the garage. I was a bit startled. He had a fairly long white beard, overalls, and an old cowboy hat on, and he just sort of stared at me. I introduced myself as I walked toward him, but it was when I got to the edge of the garage where he was that things got just a little uncomfortable. Behind him at the other corner of the garage was who I suppose was his son, half visible around the corner, mid-thirties I would guess, also, long beard, overalls, worn hat, and standing just at the edge of the garage. I didn't hear banjo music, but it wouldn't have surprised me if I had. The old man didn't say much, and neither did I at this point. I told him ever

---

. B London Jr. and Neil B. Wiseman, *The Heart of a Great Pastor* (Ventura, Regal Books, 1994), 51.

so briefly about our church and backed myself out to my car. But you have to try.

Learning your people and community is essential in loving them. I have never been good at just walking up to a door and knocking on it. Same way with evangelism—I've just never been comfortable with it. And so it is with visiting people for church. I prefer to call and make appointments, and I have found that people appreciate that. For example, while in Bonham I was planning to visit a family that had come to our church. I called them and set up a good time to come by. One of our deacons went with me (a great practice—this allows you to spend time with deacons in one-on-one settings and also gets them to visiting). As we sat in the living room, the wife thanked us for calling before coming over. She told us that another church in town that they had visited had begun to come visit them. They would just show up, and from what she said at very inopportune times. Once she answered the door early on a Saturday morning in her nightgown, and once they were all as a family walking out the door to go somewhere. She said it got to the point she told her husband to call the church and tell them not to come back to their house. She was very grateful that we took their family schedule into account in calling to see when a convenient time would be to visit.

While I was in Texarkana at Highland Park from 1997–2001, the man who taught our young married Sunday school class and I were hoping to find some prospects from among the members of the class, their friends and such. Randy taught the class and told me about a conversation from one Sunday morning. He was talking to the class about their friends as possible prospects, and no one was giving him any names. He pressed a little more, and finally one of the couples spoke up. Apparently, they did not want to give any names because they didn't want him and the pastor going to visit their friends. They were afraid of what we would think of their homes and did not want to put their friends in an awkward situation. It was as though they thought we would be doing a home inspection and would be judging their friends. And to take it a step closer, the members of the class really didn't even want me visiting in their homes, and they were church members! They were just uncomfortable with the pastor coming into their home. No matter how we tried to convince them we just wanted to get to know them better and see how we could minister to them and love them, they just didn't want us coming over.

Now, on the other end of the age spectrum, senior adults for the most part love for you to drop in on them. I think it will be very interesting to see if this trend changes as the current thirty- to forty-year-olds get into their sixties and up. I hope Ed Stetzer and Thom Rainer[7] are still around to give us the statistics on that in the next few years.

I still made it a practice of calling before I just showed up and found that every time I did so, the person was very grateful that I was courteous of his or her time and situation. I found that it also set the person at ease a little more. I would let people know when I called I just wanted to come by and see how they were doing and visit for a short time. This allowed them to not be worried about why the pastor may be coming over.

It is so important that you get to know your church members. And you can only do that by spending time among them. Study the first several chapters of Nehemiah and you will not only find a great lesson on spiritual leadership, but note the times he comments, "I was among the people," "we were," and things like that. As you learn about them and their family, make mental notes and remember. Believe me, when one of their children or grandchildren come to town and show up at church and you can

---

Ed Stetzer is president of LifeWay Research. Thom Rainer is president CEO of Lifeway Christian Resources.

call them by name, it makes quite an impression on your church member. You have shown them that you were listening, and it is a way of saying that you love them.

There was another practice I had while pastoring, and this is much easier to do when you are in a church that runs three hundred or less. I made a concerted effort to make some kind of physical contact with every person who came to each service—shaking hands, a pat on the back, or gentle touch to the shoulder. I am not a big hugger, and I just felt I needed to be careful with that sort of contact. You will have those ladies who want a hug from their pastor, and that is fine. Just have some discernment with who and how you hug. Be sure you are giving high fives to the children. They love that. It brings a personal touch. It was during these times that I was also able to ask folks about things they were dealing with and things they had shared with me or mentioned during Wednesday night prayer meeting or other times. Again, when you remember something like that, it lets them know you care, you are listening, and you love them.

I think that every pastor is told this, and you read this in a lot of books, so I will add it here to make sure you see it again: when you first go to a church, don't change anything. No, seriously, don't change anything! Spend the first months, six months to a year, just preaching the Word and loving the people. I heard Frank Page say in a conference one time that your first year you should be loving, listening, and learning.[8] That is great advice. Get to know the people, listen to them, learn about them, learn about the church, and learn about the community. When you have shown the people that you are there to love and serve them, and have

---

[8] Bluebonnet Baptist Association Leadership Conference, First Baptist Church Canyon Lake. April 3, 2014. Dr. Frank Page is president and chief executive officer of the Southern Baptist Convention Executive Committee.

proven it by spending time with them, then when the appropriate time to make some changes comes, you will have the support of the people. Don't take this wrong—it is not a manipulation tactic. If you go about it like that, the people will see through it. And your plans for change will be met with opposition, and worse, you may start to receive U-Haul gift certificates in the mail.

I'm dating myself here, and if you have never heard of him you can Google it. Singer B. J. Thomas, who had a fantastic voice, sang a song back in 1979 titled "Using Things and Loving People." The song started out with this verse:

Using things and loving people, That's the way it's got to be. Using things and loving people, Look around and you can see, That loving things and using people Only leads to misery.[9]

You will find that there are people who are easier to love than others. Love the difficult people anyway. Rick Warren says that in every church there are people he considers "EGR" people, "Extra Grace Required."[10] This is true. When I went to preach in view of a call in Bonham, I was told by a couple of people on the committee that on that Sunday morning there would most likely be about sixty people in attendance and probably four would vote against me. Well, there were sixty-four ballots turned in, and the vote was sixty in favor and four opposed. It's just the way they were.

I believe that it cannot be said loud enough and seriously enough that when you go to a church, no matter what you have heard about "those few people," you love everyone there the same. You go in with a clean slate in reference to the people. I have always been the type to want to give everyone the benefit of

---

[9] Written by: Archie Paul Jordan, Hal David. Lyrics © Universal Music Publishing Group. From the album "You Gave Me Love" 1979

[10] Rick Warren, *The Purpose Driven Life*. (Grand Rapids, MI: Zondervan Publishing, 2002), 149.

the doubt, to look for and find the best in people. Honestly there have been a few who challenged that. Love them anyway. There were a few times with a few people that I literally had to force them to shake my hand, but I would smile at them and as best I could treat them with the same love and respect as the person who admired me the most.

It has been interesting to see that upon arriving at a couple of churches and being "warned" about "those members" that I would take that information with a grain of salt and let them prove themselves. Several of those instances I never had a bit of trouble with or from that "trouble church member." And a few of those became great supporters of mine where they had not supported a previous pastor. So approach your new church setting with the goal of loving the people, listen, take note of warnings you may be given, but don't let that cause you to target or avoid anyone.

Another element to loving the people, and this is somewhat determined by the community you will be in, but be loving in the community. Again, I will use my own personal experiences. I've already mentioned a little about the area around the church in Magnolia. It was a low-income area, with a lot of needs. As you meet people around the church, you are able to learn about them and some of their needs. When and as you are able, seek to meet the needs of the people, whether they come to your church or not. My wife and I did this several times as we were able to, and it makes an impact. In Bonham, we did this by getting out in the community and getting involved. My wife opened an upscale children's clothing store just off the town square. Dating us a bit again, just remember I'm old. She named the store Watercolor Ponies after the great Wayne Watson song.[11] Google him. If

---

[11] Wayne Watson, "Watercolour Ponies" from the album by the same name, Dayspring Records, 1987. www.waynewatson.com

you are not familiar with the song, it talks about how quickly your children grow up and "ride away." Helps to have a Kleenex handy as you listen. Anyway, owning the store allowed her to get involved with the businesspeople in town and to meet people from the area. I'm not necessarily recommending you get your spouse to open a business, but working in the community was a plus. I helped coach my son's little league baseball team. Also, and this is something that I haven't found since leaving Bonham in 1997, we had a great fellowship among the other pastors in the area.

This helps in a number of ways that this little book is not taking on. Suffice it to say, you need to build relationships with other pastors in your area. Back on topic, spending time with the other pastors was not merely good for me and each of us, but it also showed the community that we loved each other and were not competing with each other. This allowed us to get to know members of other churches, which just builds the ministry for all the churches. It showed the members of our churches that we truly cared for the community and wanted what was best for all of them. It's a matter of loving people.

In Texarkana our church was next to an elementary school. I made it a point to volunteer in the school. I would read in classrooms and serve as a monitor at lunch and mentored a little boy one school year. My son was in the school, and so from time to time as my wife was working, Logan would after school come over to the church. I would stand outside as school was about to let out and wait for him. This gave me the opportunity to meet parents who were picking up their children and also visit with the teachers.

This next idea I borrowed from First Baptist Church Magnolia and Dr. Ed Seay as they did this for the school district Magnolia. Because Highland Park Baptist Church at the time wasn't a large congregation, we targeted just the elementary school next door, which was called Highland Park Elementary. One year before school started, as the teachers were coming back that week before the students, we hosted them all for lunch. Our folks did a wonderful job of preparing a great meal. We decorated the fellowship hall, we had some door prizes, and we invited the entire faculty over for a relaxing off-campus lunch. It was a blessing to them. It showed them we cared about them, and several of the teachers began attending our church because of this.

In DeKalb loving the community was much easier because DeKalb is a small town. One person told me soon after I began there that one of the things you do in DeKalb to be out in the community is go outside at night and if you see lights, go to the lights. What was happening? Something was going on at the city park, and that's where the people would be. DeKalb also had several large town events throughout the year, and so as I could I would plug in to those. "Saturday in the Park"—yes, it's an awesome song by the group Chicago, but in this case it referred to the last Saturday in September. This was an all-day event at the city park that began with groups spending the night Friday night and working on their chili for the chili cook-off. There was an all-day softball tournament, a volleyball tournament, stick horse races, pet show, donut-eating competition, and homemade ice cream, of which on two occasions I was honored to be a judge. (Being involved in the community does have some perks.) This day was also the set up for Octoberfest, which is always the first Saturday in October. There was a huge parade, and I am serious when I say a huge parade. For the size of the town this parade is seriously larger than other big towns I've been in. Vendors line the streets, and there is a kid's carnival, all day singing, an ar' show, and a variety show. It is a great day in DeKalb, Texas.

guess this could be a plug for it if you are ever in Northeast Texas the first of October, I recommend you go.)

As a pastor, you mingle, you walk slowly through the crowd, and you sit and visit with folks. And then there is high school football. Need I say more? One of the pastors, Steve McMichael, a dear friend of mine, and I spent a lot of time praying together through those eleven years. Well, Pastor Steve is the voice of DeKalb Bear football. He announces the games. And I would on occasion go up in the press box and be a spotter for him. Because our middle son, Logan, and then daughter, Lauren, were in the band, I would announce the band at halftime. I would say that Pastor Steve is really the town's pastor. He has been the pastor at Maranatha Christian Center for over twenty-five years! And if there is an event going on, you will see Brother Steve and his sweet wife, Mechele. He loves the community, he loves the people, and they know it! It's being involved. The pastor who followed me at First Baptist, Brother James Sparks, along with another member of the church do radio broadcasts of the football games. It's being involved in and for the community.

There were occasions in DeKalb where I just needed to get out of the office. You will have those days. Either writer's block hits you, or you have studied so much you can't think, or maybe something is weighing heavy on your heart. That's when you go for a walk. So I would literally walk down the main business street in DeKalb. (There's really only one; it's a small town.) I would go in the businesses and just say hello to the folks and see how they were doing. No agenda, just to say hello and encourage folks.

One of the best things, in my opinion, we did was something I got from Houston Northwest one Christmas. That church is located on FM 249, which is also called the Tomball Parkway. One year they put on a large outdoor Christmas production called *ickens on the Parkway.* The lot behind the church was turned into a turn-of-the-century town with all kinds of little vignettes. We dressed in turn-of-the-century outfits, and people could walk through the event. Well, Dan Blocker is from DeKalb, again Google. Dan Blocker played Hoss Cartwright on the old western *Bonanza*. (Google it, young people.)

When I learned this and drove to DeKalb for an interview with the pastor search committee, I saw a lot next to the church. I was told the church owned the lot, and the idea hit me, "Christmas on the Ponderosa." (The Ponderosa was what the Cartwrights called their place—again Google.) And so after I arrived I began talking about the idea. It caught on, and December 2001 we held the first of two "Christmas on the Ponderosa," and it was a great event. We built an old west town, even had a sawdust path for people to walk around. There was a bake shop complete with homemade goods for sale, a blacksmith shop with men actually doing some work, an outdoor café that served chili, stew, cornbread, hot chocolate, and coffee. We had a theater where our youth group did a puppet show. There was the store front with a porch and rocking chair, and at one point during the night a member read the story to children, *T'was the Night before Christmas—in Texas, That Is.* Our young adult class built a long slide that was a "snow sled ride." We had a stage where some folks sang at different times of the night. In the middle of the lot we had a church house set up. To begin the evening events, our minister of music and I rode in on horseback with western outfits. We even wore long slickers, and we started the evening off with a brief church service. All the money raised from the sale of food went to the Lottie Moon Christmas Offering for International Missions. It was quite an event. We had it for three days even though one evening was rained out. The second year we did this, we had people drive in from up to fifty miles away. One lady in town told me that second year that she was so hopin we were doing it again because it was just a great way to begin the holidays. Loving the community.

Perhaps the best thing we did all the years I was in DeKalb that got the most responses from is that we began the "Welcome Back Teacher Appreciation Lunch." It was like that we did in Texarkana, only with our church size in DeKalb, we were able to host the entire school district and also two smaller schools in communities within a few miles of DeKalb. Again, the church folks were amazing at providing some great food. Our church's administrative assistant, Pam Prather, did a fantastic job at decorating the Family Life Center. We had businesses in town that would donate door prizes, and the first couple of years I had a guest speaker come in to encourage the teachers. We would put paper on the tables and lay out crayons and pens and pencils for the teachers to play tic-tac-toe or connect the dots, but what they began doing was writing thank-you notes to the church for the lunch.

After a couple of years, I was asked by a few of the teachers if we would consider not having a guest speaker. They enjoyed that but, for some of them it was the first time they had seen each other since the previous year, and they just enjoyed relaxing and talking. One less thing I had to plan. I was good with that. It worked. Time and time again I would be told how much they were looking forward to the lunch as the summer was winding down. On several occasions, a new teacher would come to me and tell me that one of the first things they were told about in coming to the district was the luncheon we provided and they had been excited about coming. There were different ways we would do the door prizes—a sticker under certain chairs, a ribbon on a spoon, after a few years the veterans would come in and before sitting down they would examine the seating to see if they could figure out what chair would get them a door prize! It was annually one of the best events we held, and we did it to tell these folks in our school district that we appreciated them, were praying for them, and we loved them. It made an impact.

Another thing we did as a group of churches was after each home football game host a "Fifth Quarter." I am sure you are familiar with these. We would host them along the main street in town and would usually have a band and free pizza. As a pastor, you walked among the teenagers, talked to them. Yes, occasionally you policed a few situations, but we would always do it with love.

There are endless ways to show people you love them, but it cannot be done without being among them. Talk with them, but more than that listen to them. Learn about the people and love them. Your loving them will build lifelong relationships and will cause them to respect you and trust you, and that allows you to minister to them. And then, as you are preaching the Word to them, they will listen to you and God will do great things in their lives.

Those two pieces of advice will carry you a long way in ministry. They served me well for twenty years. The next four things come from me. I'm sure you can find them written about by someone somewhere. I've honestly not seen them in any book I've read the way I will write about it, but that doesn't mean someone else hasn't thought about it also. I'm not that profound a thinker. These are four things that I have observed and so put into place in my life. Again, they have helped me. I will say that Dr. Jimmy Draper addresses a couple of them to an extent in his newest book, which I highly recommend, *Don't Quit Before You Finish*.[12] Get that book, read it, study it, and highlight it. I wish he had written it around 1990 so I could have had it

---

[12] Dr. Jimmy Draper, *Don't Quit Before You Finish* (Franklin, TN: Clovercroft Publishing, 2015).

from the beginning of my ministry. I need to give credit to Dr. Draper. It was reading that book earlier this month (March 2016) that spurred my thinking into this writing project. I had the privilege of having Dr. Draper in our church in DeKalb twice and the opportunity to interact with him for a few years. He is a wonderful, loving man of God. Get that book! While some of what I will say in these next two chapters is written about in his book, he does a more thorough job of discussing it in certain ways.

Chapter 3

GIVE NO CAUSE TO BE CONSIDERED LAZY

I'm going to write about these in the order I have learned them through my years of ministry. It would I think make more sense to have written about the subject of chapter 5 as chapter 1, but I wanted to begin with the first bits of advice I was given, so just keep reading please.

What do I mean with the title of this chapter? It's simple, yet incredibly serious. Don't give anyone any reason to consider you as lazy. And I'm not necessarily talking about laying around the house on your day off watching sports. This needs to be taken to apply to every arena of your life. Let's begin with the preaching and teaching ministry you have. I referenced earlier a young pastor one time telling me he didn't have time to prepare for a Wednesday night Bible study. As I said and I will repeat, there is essentially no excuse for this. As a minister of the Lord Jesus Christ, you are to be giving your all to Him and for Him. If you haven't got that one yet, you need to close this book and do some serious business with the Lord. Go ahead, I'll wait.

Now that you're on the right page, let's think about this. For way too long the joke about preachers has been that we only work one day a week and yet when we do that we work too long. Ha, ha, ha … There are two groups of you who will be reading this, possibly three. First those of you who will serve in a more traditional format church. By that I mean you will be preaching a Sunday morning service, a Sunday evening service, and a Wednesday evening service. To some of you that is already a foreign concept. Trust me, there are plenty of churches still around who hold and expect three preaching services a week. Second, there are those of you who will have a Sunday morning service and a Wednesday night service, no Sunday night because you are really up to date. And then believe it or not, third, and I know of a few, some of you will serve in churches that only have a Sunday morning preaching service. Now, you may lead a small group some other time during the week but still only one preaching service.

Now does the point of this chapter make a little more sense?

For those of you in churches with only one or two preaching services, that's a lot of time you don't have to spend studying and writing. What are you going to do? And my goodness if you are not preaching amazing sermons that one or two times a week, something is tragically wrong. Consider this—there are many pastors out there, I was one of them, who taught a Sunday school class, preached three new sermons a week, and occasionally led a discipleship class all at the same time. I also led a service at the local nursing home once a month and led a Bible study at the courthouse for a group of people during their lunch break once a month. That was in the midst of all the other duties that come with being a pastor—oh yes, and a husband and father of three. So time management is a very important part of your life, and with that study and sermon writing must have a priority spot.

I've already included 2 Timothy 2:15 earlier, "be diligent." Another way to say it, "don't be lazy." And here's the thing—when you are lazy in your preparation, the people in the pew will know it. I am not sure who first said it, many people have quoted it, to name a couple Dr. Howard Hendricks of Dallas Theological Seminary,[13] also Chuck Swindoll.[14] The quote from Chuck is from an article by Rick Warren. Anyway here it is: "A mist in the pulpit leads to a fog in the pew." You must, you must put in the time with your sermons. Another thing, and I have seen this over the past few years with younger preachers, don't get your sermon online. Don't memorize someone else's; write your own stuff. Have I ever preached someone else's sermon? Yes, sort of. I'll explain. When Rick Warren's *40 Days of Purpose* came out, we went through it in DeKalb. I used Rick's outlines for the sermons, but I filled in my own material.

One Sunday night I read a sermon, Jonathan Edwards's great "Sinners in the hands of an angry God."[15] Every Christian needs to read or hear that one. And then fairly recently, as I have mentioned the man I refer to as "my pastor," Brother Billy Crosby, back in 1983 preached what is to me still the greatest sermon I have ever heard, "One More Night With the Frogs." I have the cassette and have always thought of learning it and preaching it. So I did, last year. I changed a bit here and there, made it more of my own, and preached it. The church taped it for me, and I sent a copy to Brother Billy. He said I did well. The interesting thing, he told me it wasn't his originally. A preacher friend of his preached it and he got it from him. He got the points to it from a preaching magazine. Keep in mind that would have been a magazine from back in the 1950s! But all in all, I always studied, prayed, even pleaded with God, and wrote my own sermons. Do I use illustrations or teaching explanations from others? Of course—I'd say you are a fool if you don't. In fact,

---

[13] http://www.missionfrontiers.org/issue/article/the-measure-of-a-ministry

[14] http://pastors.com/real-purpose-preaching-matters/

[15] http://www.gutenberg.org/files/34632/34632-h/34632-h.htm#Page_78

this morning on the way to the office I was listening to Chuck Swindoll (which I highly recommend you do), and he shared something about the resurrection of Jesus that I had never heard before. It came from an old book he had read. It was a fantastic point about the grave clothes Jesus left behind. Will I use it? You bet I will. For one thing Chuck Swindoll can be trusted! That's an important point—be careful who you study from. Make sure they are scholars, experts in theology and doctrine. And with who you listen to, if they are influencing you, make sure they are good orators. That is, make sure they aren't boring. Look, being boring is not a spiritual gift. Learn to deliver the sermon well. There are those who will say you are not in the pulpit to "entertain" people. I beg to differ. According to Webster, one of the entries in the definition of the word "entertain" is this: "to hold in mind."[16] The idea here is to grab people's attention and be able to hold their attention. Young preacher, if you are not grabbing and holding the attention of the congregation, they are not getting it. I do not mean to be a stand-up comic, or a motivational speaker with overdone and fake emotions, nor do I discount the power and movement of the Holy Spirit. You must be you, but you need to learn to deliver the sermon well.

So, the best studying you will ever do is when you get alone with the Lord, surrender yourself to the Holy Spirit, and study the Bible. Along with that, learn all you can with scholarly professors. Read and listen to those men that have been effectively preaching and teaching the Word of God for many years. I could give you a list of my favorites, but you need to find your own. "Be diligent" about your study. Don't give anyone any possible chance at saying that when it comes to studying and preaching that you are lazy. Be prepared. Have a word from the Lord for the people He has

---

[16] *Webster's New Dictionary of the English Language.* (New York: The Popular Group, LLC. 2005), 164.

allowed you to stand before. I have always felt that in my time as a pastor, and even now as a director of missions, when given the chance to preach, my primary responsibility is to help people hear from God through His Word. That doesn't come from cute, witty sayings that I come up with or funny stories in an effort to make a point. Preach the Word with diligence.

How does this flesh out for you? That is up to you. How much time does it take to prepare a good sermon? A young pastor once asked an older pastor this question, and the older pastor responded, "About ten years." While looking for the source of that quote (which I could not find), I came across a good article on the website "Pastoralized" and have included the web address in the footnotes.[17] Thom Rainer wrote about this in one of his blogs where he conducted what he called an "unscientific poll." I have included that web address in the footnotes also.[18] Now, the longer I have been in ministry, the more I understand the comment about it taking ten years. But as a young pastor, don't let that discourage you. In fact, that should encourage you. The longer you are at the practice, the art of writing sermons, the more biblical truths you will be gathering as you study, which helps you as you prepare. Every pastor has his method, every pastor has his time frame, and I would even add to that depending on the text determines the time it takes to put the sermon together. I would say that you shouldn't even have a time frame in your mind. For example, to say, "I need to spend fifteen to twenty hours this week on Sunday morning and ten to fifteen on Sunday night ..." You pray, read, study, and write until you complete the sermon. Then as you review it you may tweak it here and there.

[17] http://www.pastoralized.com/2013/09/26/the-number-of-hours-keller-piper-driscoll-and-5-others-spend-on-sermon-prep/

[18] http://thomrainer.com/2013/06/how-much-time-do-pastors-spend-preparing-a-sermon/

Always allow the Holy Spirit to guide you through the process. I remember one time hearing this, and I have often found it to be true. There are three sermons you preach for every sermon you preach. There is the one you practice, the one you actually preach, and then the one you wish you would have preached. Sometimes this is so true—usually it was on Monday mid-morning that the thought hit me of what I didn't say that I wish I would have ...

There are times when a sermon will come together literally in a matter of minutes. A good friend of mine, Pastor Dr. Jeff Schreve of the First Baptist Church in Texarkana, Texas, we have known each other since junior high school. Anyway, his favorite movies are the *Rocky* movies starring Sylvester Stallone. Did you know that Stallone wrote the screenplay for the first *Rocky*[19] movie in only three and half days! What's the point? Think about that, three and half days to write a screenplay for a two-hour movie! Some movies take weeks and months to write.

Same with sermons. Some I have literally had come together in less than an hour, others I have worked on for weeks before they were complete. It is a labor of love. Don't be lazy when it comes to your study and preparation. Dig in to the text, and when you need to, dig into the Hebrew and Greek. So often our English language just does not capture what the original language is saying. You have to go to the study tools to see a little more— sometimes a lot more. I don't want to get into a language lecture here. You have textbooks for that. The emphasis I am making is that sermon writing is work, and you must not be lazy when it comes to your preaching.

Now let me take you to a thought that perhaps you haven't considered. Remember, the point of this chapter is not doing anything that would give anyone a reason to consider you lazy.

---

[19] https://www.nytimes.com/packages/html/movies/bestpictures/ rocky-ar.html

Please read me well. I am not trying to toot my own horn, and I am not bragging in any sense. I want you to learn from what I have experienced that served me well. And I could give you names and numbers of people who would back this up. I hope that isn't necessary and you will believe what I am sharing with you. (Proofreading I had the thought that this little paragraph may cause you to think, *Well, if this is the case why are you not still pastoring? Don't you know the old adage, "Those that can, do, those that can't teach."* I decided to share how it was that I left the pastorate to move into associational work in the appendix. Hope you will take the time to read that also.)

Here's the example I will give, a couple of them. The first small church I pastored in Magnolia was a struggling church in a struggling area. The area has since grown and is beautiful. When I was there the church consisted of three portable buildings. Now they have a beautiful building. When I was there the area around the church was made up of three very low-income mobile home parks. Today there are estates of three to five acres, all of which have high-dollar horses roaming the properties. While I was there I not only preached, and bless their hearts, I have looked through some of those old sermons. I feel sorry for those people having to listen to me. I trust I improved through the years. Anyway, back to the point. I preached, yes, but I also cleaned the church and mowed the yard, and on several occasions I got up extra early drove to First Baptist Magnolia and picked up their church van, then drove the ten or so miles out to Silver Springs and drove the neighborhoods picking up children for church. You just do what needs to be done.

In Bonham, Texarkana, and DeKalb after fellowships I would always be quick to begin picking up trash, grabbing a broom or mop, and getting busy. One of the things I would do in DeKalb as the fellowship meals were winding down is I would go to the kitchen and get a large cooking pot. Then I would begin picking up the cups that still had some tea in them and dumping the tea in the large pot and throwing away the cup. When the pot was full, I would take it outside and dump it, come in, and start over. When chairs and tables need to be moved, jump in and help. When we went on construction mission trips, I was not going to be seen standing around or supervising. Whatever I could do that needed to be done, I would do it, whether that meant the important part of using the nail gun to build a wall, going to get more nails for the guy who was using the nail gun, or picking up scraps and trash around the build site. You just do what needs to be done. Don't give anyone any reason to consider you lazy.

Why? Because if you are lazy about helping out with fellowships, if you are lazy on mission trips, it will be assumed you are lazy about study and life in general. And I want to add something here. In DeKalb there is (still is) an amazing kitchen committee—I mean amazing. In DeKalb we had a full-time custodian. That didn't stop me from picking up candy wrappers and extra bulletins in the sanctuary, emptying trash cans, straightening up, sweeping, mopping, tables, chairs. I wanted to be in there helping and being a part of it.

While I was in DeKalb, we built an education building that attached to the back of the sanctuary and then ran parallel to the office building. In between the two buildings and close to the parking lot we had a load of rocks dumped to be spread. I will admit that I watched the pile of rocks sit for about two weeks, just a bit of an experiment. And then one Saturday I took my shovel. We lived in the parsonage right next to (and I do mean right next to) the church. I began to spread the rocks. At that time we had some old chairs that we were giving to another church in the area, a church that one of our members used to attend. This church member, Kent, drove up, and two men from the other church pulled up behind him with their truck and a trailer.

They got out, and Kent came over to see me and introduce me to the men. "Guys, this is Brother Walter, my pastor."

One of the men, shaking my hand, looked at Kent and said, "This is your pastor?"

Kent said, "Yes it is."

This is the honest truth—the man looked back at me and said with a serious look on his face, "You are the first pastor I have ever seen using a shovel."

Reader, that is a sad commentary on preachers. It thrilled Kent, and he told the man of other things he had been involved with me doing around the church, but it made me a bit sad that the man had a certain view of preachers. Another example is from while the building was being constructed. The retired builders came to build the inside of the building, and several of the days I had on my work clothes and tool belt and joined in. One of the older men—actually they were all older men—told me I was the first pastor to pick up a hammer and help out on a build.

In that new building we had a coffee bar at the entrance, and I would get over there on Sunday mornings before anyone else and make coffee so it would be hot and ready as people began to arrive. And I don't even drink coffee.

I have known guys in the ministry who amazed me at how they could get out of doing physical labor. Don't be that guy. Whether it is as simple as picking up bulletins, candy wrappers, and used Kleenex after the service, or standing on ceiling joists holding up the beams for a roof on a mission trip or working with disaster relief, emptying cups of tea or moving chairs and tables, be a part of the life of your church.

Another arena to consider with this relates back to the previous chapter. Don't be lazy when it comes to the important task of visiting your congregation and reaching out to prospects. This takes effort, which means it also takes time. And I have just spoken of a great deal of time that needs to be given to your preparation. In the next paragraph I am going to bring up another subject to add to your list ... Yes, it goes on and on. That is the nature of ministry. Some of you will be fortunate enough to serve in churches with multiple staff, which means there are others who can help with the hospital visiting, nursing homes, prospects, and other situations. But pastor, you will find that in your church there will be people who don't think they have had a real visit if you don't go see them. I remember one older lady in one of the churches I served who was in the hospital for a day or two. I don't remember the reason, but I was not able to get to the hospital to see her. I heard about it later—boy did I hear about it! The thing is she was visited by several members of her Sunday school class, two deacons saw her, and another of our pastoral staff did as well. But I didn't, so she made sure word got back to me that she didn't get visited while in the hospital. Really? Yes, that is a true story! Be diligent in your sermon preparation, be diligent in helping out where needed, and be diligent in your pastoral ministry. Now here's another one.

Don't be lazy when it comes to your family! But there are only twenty-four hours in a day! And you have just poured on me about the sermon writing and the helping out around the church and then the pastoral ministry and now you are reminding me about family? I know that, and every one of us have the same twenty-four hours of the day. This is a serious subject, and I would encourage you to ask every pastor who is older than you how he does it. I'm not saying that my method is "the" way to go about it. My wife and I have three children who are all grown now. And so here now is that moment of bragging. We have a beautiful six-and-a-half-year-old granddaughter, Lillyann, who is our oldest child, Landon, and his wife, Wendy's. And then our youngest is our daughter, Lauren. She is married to Dionicio, and they as of the writing of this book have a two-month-old little boy, Ezekiel. Our middle child, Logan, is at the moment still single (but we are hopeful). I remember reading biographies of the great evangelist Billy Sunday, and that because of his zealousness and commitment to ministry and the intense preaching schedule he kept, his relationships with his children suffered greatly.[20] When I was single, I vowed to not let that happen. So I determined that when I was at home, I was going to be Dad at home. Yes, we taught our kids to memorize scripture as they were growing up, and yes we had family devotions. But I will confess at this point that we did not—no, let me rephrase that, I did not keep family devotions as I should have through the years. I recommend you do. I believe I let my family down along the way in that. I wanted to be Dad to them, not preacher Dad. I have heard the stories from both sides. There are those who were strict and disciplined about family devotion time and family Bible study time and even rigid in some areas. And there were those who didn't really do anything we would consider spiritual with the family away from church. With both sides of this, I have known of children who grew up never being a problem, loving the Lord and the church, and serving in the church as they grew. They are now grown adults and have continued to serve the Lord. I have also heard of those parents (even pastors' families) who struggled with their children, problems and trouble, rebellion, and even run-ins with the law. Some are prodigals, some of whom came home later in life, and others never did. I wish there was an easy answer to this one. You already know that your family will live under a microscope, will be scrutinized often without any consideration

---

[20] http://www.newworldencyclopedia.org/entry/Billy_Sunday. (This is but one brief description of the life of his children.)

of mercy, will be the object of gossip and sometimes even be the targets of attack. It comes with the territory. Don't be lazy when it comes to giving them your time, especially when your kids are young. I was looking through my journal for that date on the question I had posed to those two older pastors, and I came across an entry on our daughter's birthday. Here is the entry:

> Thursday, 26th Happy birthday, Lauren! Number two. Stayed home to have a tea party with Lauren and her new kitchen set.

Men, you have to do this. I was reminded as well reading entries of the times I left the office early to take the boys fishing, where there were little league baseball games, and then here is an important one, vacations. This may sound strange, but I would stress that you are diligent with a day off and with taking vacations. Your family needs this from you. As your children are young, they understand your love for them in your time with them. As they get older, your kids relate your love for them by, yes, your time with them. Be diligent to love your kids.

Now let's not forget your wife. This is sort of adding up, isn't it? Sermon preparation, helping out around the church, pastoral ministry, and I haven't even addressed the administrative responsibility—don't forget that part of it—then children and now wife also? Twenty-four hours in a day, right?

Your wife will be your biggest supporter. You are a team in this even if she doesn't hold a position in the church. When I was meeting with the people at Silver Springs in Magnolia, Lisa was as the Bible would say "great with child." She was six months pregnant with Logan and already uncomfortable. We were sitting in the church when one of the wives looked at Lisa and said, "And what will you be doing in the church?" Lisa, in the way that only she can, paused, then looked down at her belly, then looked up and said, "I think I am going to have a baby." Through the years Lisa taught Sunday school classes from young girls to senior adult ladies, led children's choir, hosted luncheons, sang in the choir, all those preacher's wife sort of things. Although she doesn't play the piano. And remember on top of things like this, your wife, like mine, may also hold an outside-the-home job, all the while raising the kids and all that goes along with living in a house! Be diligent about giving her your time. It's not always easy, but you have to make time to sit and talk, and not always about church things. In fact, there were many, many things I never told Lisa about what was going on at church because I did not want her stressed over it. She was and still is my greatest defender and supporter, and I could not have done any of it without her by my side. She deserves my time.

You have to set your own boundaries, but set them, and let the church know what they are. I made sure from the very beginning that the church knew that my family came first. And you know what? The churches I served respected that. Sure, there are going to be people who don't like that you may miss some meeting or event because your son has a little league game, but they will get over it. And even if they don't, what is more important to you, that a church member is mad that you missed their event or that your son didn't see you in the stands at his ball game? I'm going with family on this one. I know that in some way some of you will read this and think I am being a bit harsh or cold—just the opposite. I wanted the church to see in me that family is important.

It's a lot like letting your kids know that you love your wife, and the best way for them to have that security is to see you loving your wife. Don't get carried away with that comment. Lisa and I did as much as we could, especially as the kids were young, to let them see us hugging and kissing and tickling each other. Sure, it embarrassed them, but that was the point! But in the midst of their, "Oh Dad, stop it, gross!" The one thing they knew, we love each other, and at the end of the day I would be coming home to them. That, my friend, is the best sermon on love your kids will ever see. Be diligent to love your family by giving them your time. And maybe I should add here if it hasn't come through clear enough, give them your best time, not your worn-out, left over time. They will know the difference.

I want to add here that these words concerning your family can have another reality to them that you desperately need to consider. Setting borders for your family is important for their protection. These same borders are important for your protection and that of your marriage. It is an unfortunate reality that ministry marriages fail, and some fail due to unfaithfulness. Yes, I know personally some that have. Yours doesn't have to. By being diligent in spending time, quality time with your wife and children, you will help maintain that safeguard against the sometimes-subtle attack of the enemy. Do not be lazy or careless when it comes to your marriage and family. Your wife is a gift from the Lord, so treat her as such. Your children are a gift from the Lord. Treat them as such.

All right, summary: sermon preparation, physically helping out, and with that, not only if you are asked to help, just help, pastoral ministry, all the administrative responsibility that I didn't touch on, and then family. Be diligent about giving this your best, don't give anyone any reason to consider you as lazy.

Let me say again that I am not giving you these personal examples to be bragging, please don't hear that as you read this. I am sharing with you these things because I have not seen this in other books to preachers, and I certainly don't remember being taught this kind of thing in seminary. Twenty-plus years of experience has taught me this, positively and negatively. Some of it I have learned the hard way. Please, please don't travel that road. To mention Rick Warren again, I love what he says about how no one has the time to learn everything the hard way. Learn from other people's mistakes. But also as is my desire with this, learn from the good things some of us older guys have experienced.

Chapter 4

DON'T BE A MOOCH

That may look strange as a title for a chapter in a book written to preachers. But again there are a few examples I want to share with you about this. And while this will be a very brief chapter, I believe it to be critically important.

There are three areas I want to address with you concerning this. The first one you will no doubt see at some time or another and most probably in every church you serve during fellowship dinners. There is always, it seems, that one person in the church who goes back for more and more. In one of the churches I served in there was a man who, regardless of the event, regardless of the other people around, he was going to be first in line for the meal. Children, elderly, guests, didn't matter, he was first in line. And that guy could get more on a plate than anyone I have ever seen.

Now, this guy wasn't homeless and wasn't really lacking for things. He wasn't rich, but he wasn't destitute either. He would pile his plate high, and then after everyone had been through the line, he would be back for seconds. And then, when it seemed all had eaten, he would head to the kitchen find the take-home containers and go back through the line to fill that up as well. And yes, you could see the eye rolls from a number of people in

Dr. Walter C. Jackson

the fellowship hall. You will have some who, when you go out to eat as a group, after the meal ask for a take-home container and then ask folks around the table if they want their leftovers. Yes, it happens.

Have there been times when we lacked for things? Oh yes, my first full-time position was as a youth minister in McAllen, Texas. Because I had not served in a full-time position before, the church (well, probably a few of the leaders) determined that I needed to begin on the low end of what could be considered full-time pay. Lisa wasn't working at the time, and Landon was just two years old. Things were tough. We didn't have insurance and so went to a free clinic when we had to. I learned the meaning of "gleaning" that you read about in scripture. The valley is known for its production of food. One day as we were driving home from something, we passed by a carrot field that had been harvested the day before. The field was full of people walking around picking up carrots that had missed making it into the truck. Well, since things were pretty tight for us, I looked at Lisa, pulled the car over, got out, and got to gleaning!

One thing I would not do was ask for leftovers at the church fellowship. But here's what does happen. As you are preaching the Word, loving the people, and being active in serving, you are gaining the love and respect of the people. And they will discover what you like and will know that food is a necessity and so will begin to offer it to you. Typically the way I experienced this was that when the fellowship was winding down, someone from the kitchen committee would come up to me and say, "Brother Walter, would you like some of the brisket to take home?" Well, yes, that would be awesome! Another example is that—and every preacher I know jokes about this from the pulpit when there is a meal to follow the service—a remark will be made about the dessert you hope will be there. For me it is chocolate chip cookies without nuts, brownies without nuts, and peach cobbler! And as would be the case, one of those wonderful kitchen committee folks would sneak up behind me at some point and say, "Brother Walter, there is a take-home box of cobbler set aside for you on top of the refrigerator in the kitchen, so don't forget it." Man, that is one thing I miss no longer being a pastor! The point is, don't ask for it. There will be people who take it on themselves to bless you and your family. Let them do so and be gracious and grateful about it.

Another area where being a mooch can be construed is in the way you talk about things. Here's the example. One church I served in we had someone who loved antiques. One day I was visiting in the home of an elderly member who had cancer. She told me of this and was not very happy about it. She said that a few days before this person was in her home visiting and admiring some of her antiques, so much so that comments were made that implied when she died, would she please leave those to them? That made a big impression on me, and I made a strong mental note concerning any comments I might make about the home and possessions of others. Now, there is nothing wrong with commenting on someone's things, but be careful how you do so. It is best if you feel led to, to say something along the lines of, "You have a beautiful home," or, "I love the way you have decorated your home." Don't ever say something like, "I would love to have a mantle clock like that," or whatever the object may be. Encouraging and affirming people with compliments about their home is a good thing, but just leave it at that.

The third area plays off of what was just written. There will be many of you who find yourself on the low end of the pay scale. Sometimes the church truly cannot help that. Be grateful for the privilege to serve, and trust that God knows where your mailbox is. He is your provider. There are, however, times when the powers that be in the church just think you shouldn't make much. It is a shame that too many church finance committees don't understand or have a proper perspective on pastoral salaries. It made the most sense to me when I believe it was John Maxwell who framed it this way. The pastor should be making what the businesspeople in the community around the church are making who have a comparable education and responsibility expectation. For example, if you are in a smaller community, the pastor should probably be making at least what the school principal or even superintendent is making.

Think about it—in many cases you have more education and at least an equivalent responsibility. In fact, I would argue you have more responsibility. After all, the people you are leading are volunteers. It's much easier to lead a group of people you are paying, but give those same people in the leadership position a large group of volunteers and let's see how well they lead. Well, all of that is another topic. One Sunday in DeKalb, I was standing at the back of the church as the service was about to close. One of the high school coaches who had been visiting the church had come out early because his young daughter had gotten a bit fussy. We were a couple of weeks from voting on the budget for the new year, so copies were out for people to pick up. The coach commented, "I saw the new budget and what they are paying you." At that point I cringed a bit, thinking he didn't like how much it was. Well, he didn't. He then said, "It's about $10,000 less than it should be." I was shocked and told him that if he would join the church quickly, I would put him on the finance committee. He got it. He saw my position as similar to the principal and superintendent and that the salary should reflect that.

Be grateful to the Lord you have the privilege to serve Him in the church, even when the pay doesn't match the position. But then here is what you need to guard against, and again it comes across as being sort of a mooch. Let's say one of your deacons pulls up one day in a brand new loaded up pickup and wants to show it off to you. How do you respond? The wrong way would be, "Wow, sure wish I could afford to drive something that nice." Don't. What about when someone in the church gets a great promotion and raise? "Man, that would be great, all that extra money coming in." Don't. A couple of families get together and go on a fantastic Caribbean cruise for two weeks. "I could only dream of taking my family on something like that." Don't. As hard as it may be, and as hurtful as it may feel to know that while they are the ones keeping your salary lower than it should be and spending money on themselves at will, and possibly not even tithing, determine that you will only celebrate with and for them. "Brother, that is one awesome truck. Good for you!" "Congratulations on the promotion. You deserve that, and I know you will do a great job." "Hey, make sure you take enough sunscreen on that cruise, and you better not post any pictures you wouldn't want me to see. Remember, whatever you post on social media may become sermon illustration material." Be happy for your congregation when blessings come into their lives, even if it seems they are not coming to you. Remember, your trust is in God, and He has an untold number of ways to bless you along the way.

It may seem like a little thing, but trust me, the way you behave and talk about things around church members is something they pay attention to.

I am not saying that you turn down blessings and gifts that people give you; just don't ask for them.

Chapter 5

DO NOT HAVE A PERSONAL AGENDA

I mentioned earlier that this perhaps should have been chapter 1. But I am writing these in the order I learned them. So, what does this one mean? Shouldn't you go into a church with a plan, a vision, an idea of what you want to do and what needs to be done? Yes, well, sort of.

If you are to have an agenda, make it the four previous bits of advice. Here's why: each of those four things takes the spotlight off of you and places it on the people you will be serving. The people are your agenda. I remember John Maxwell sharing in a conference I attended a story about a staff member when he was pastoring. He was standing on the sidewalk out in front of the church offices talking with some people of the church when a staff member hurried by them, hardly looking up and saying hello. John followed him to his office and then asked what he was in such a hurry about. The person replied he had a lot of work to get to, to which John replied, "You just walked right past your work." People are our work. It was John Maxwell who said in talking to preachers, "Always remember you will often do more ministry on the way to the pulpit than you will ever do in the pulpit." That goes back to why I would always try to have a personal contact with every person who came into the building before each service.

So, your agenda is to be pleasing and obedient to the Lord and love the people. I have known guys and seen guys who in going to a church had as their agenda to make the church the next great mega church. Their idea was they needed as soon as possible to change the music style. You know if you are going to be a successful church today you have to be doing contemporary praise and worship. If you are going to reach young people, you have to be doing new music. Really? And how many of those new young people who are not church types have any clue as to what kind of music is "new contemporary praise music"? Well we need to have projector and a screen and be online ... Look, all that may be well and good and help a little, but if you come in talking about all that, don't expect to stay long. Remember the comment I included earlier from H. B. London Jr.? "Bloom where you are planted."

I was once asked by a search committee what my vision for their church would be. I told them I had no idea because I had never been to their church. At first they were a bit taken back by that answer, but as it began to soak in a little, they got it.

The church is not about you, pastor. This is a good time to share with you my favorite verse of scripture, John 3:30, and it is best to review the context (it's always best to review the context). A few of John the Baptist's followers are coming to him to inform him that the crowds were all going to see Jesus. These were obviously the Sunday school director and chairman of deacons. But that is up for some debate. Anyway, John understood his place, his position, his ministry, his agenda. Start with verse twenty-seven:

John answered and said, "A man can receive nothing unless it has been given him from heaven. You yourselves are my witnesses that I said, 'I am not the Christ,' but, 'I have been sent ahead of

Him.' He who has the bride is the bridegroom; but the friend of the bridegroom, who stands and hears him, rejoices greatly because of the bridegroom's voice. So this joy of mine has been made full. (John 3:27–29)

Then we see this amazing statement, in fact it is my life verse. I confess I don't always live up to it but it is my goal:

"He (Jesus) must increase, but I (John and so me and you) must decrease."

Obviously the parentheses I added. Your agenda as pastor of the local church and any other ministry you may have is to increase Jesus.

It's not about you; it's all about Him. Your agenda needs to be to help people see Jesus, meet Jesus, know Jesus, hear from Jesus. And this is what should permeate every ministry, event, and activity that takes place in and around your church.

And I will just add a comment here regarding the previous two chapters. If you will make Jesus your agenda, it will help take care of the two previous topics. When people know that you are determined to make Jesus the reason for and center of everything about your life and ministry, it will develop and/or change the culture of the church. Now, that may take time, but if you will stay at it, it will happen.

I have a sermon I wrote not long after coming to be a director of missions, knowing that I would have the opportunity to preach in different churches. Now, as you read that try not to let the stereotype of the DOM and his preaching cause you to think such about me. You know what that is, don't you? The DOM only needs about five or six sermons that he can preach over and over just in different churches. Okay, so a little of that may be true. Anyway, my approach to preaching has changed a bit. Except for the opportunity I may have to be an interim pastor, my preaching is a one time here and another time there thing.

I have begun to look at sermon writing as how I can encourage the churches. I wrote a sermon not long after coming into this ministry that I titled "Verses to Revolutionize Your Life." It really is pretty good—just throwing that out there. I share four verses of scripture that could/should be "life verses" and how they can revolutionize your life. With them I share two things about the verse that makes it that powerful a verse. And so with John 3:30, I explain that when we let the truth of this verse get deep into us. And it is at this point I feel the need to share a personal conviction. Many times through the years I would have someone come to me and say, "Preacher, we need deeper Bible study. We just need to get deeper in the Word." I stopped believing that a long, long time ago. My reason? Most Christians know more than they are doing right now. What we need is to let what we know get deeper into us! Case in point is this verse in John. Consider these points I make with the sermon. When we let, "He must increase, but I must decrease" begin to go deep into our hearts and minds and impact the way we live, there are at least two things that happen. First of all, the truths of this verse build surrender and humility in us. I think you will agree with me that one thing that is greatly needed in the lives of church members in our churches today is surrender to the Lord and humility.

Allowing this verse to dig deep will do that. The second thing is that the truths of this verse will remove pride. Think about it—when we are making Jesus more and more and making ourselves less and less, pride has no room to grow or even remain. Do you know of any church members who need that? Don't say their names out loud please. Someone may hear you. But then again, isn't that probably a need in your own life as well? Having as your agenda the increase of Jesus in yourself and others will dramatically change the way you see ministry and the way you go about ministry. For example, with that verse in mind, think about the way you drive. Touch a nerve there? How about the way you think of the person who is in front of you at the grocery store when you have quickly run in to grab two things and get to the twenty items and less lane to see a person with a cart containing at least thirty-five items? Now remember the verse. What you want is for that person to see Jesus, not your own frustration with his or her complete lack of respect for signage. Transfer that into your church. Think of that member who seems to have a criticism and complaint about everything. A piece of your mind may be what you think that person needs, but isn't it better that he or she gets more of Jesus? So I guess I am saying that I recommend you make John 3:30 your ministry agenda. That's genuinely not a bad idea. Sort of like making the Great Commission your church vision statement rather than coming up with some catchy phrase. Just stick with scripture.

Having no personal agenda keeps you out of the spotlight. This is also helpful when people don't like your ideas. Apply this if you are locked in on an agenda of where the church needs to go, or worse, you feel must go, and then the majority of the people or at least the influencers in the church don't agree. After all, you are not from there, are you? Their rejection will sit heavy on your heart and mind, and that typically takes you nowhere good. It will lead you to feelings of failure or bitterness, neither need a place in your life.

So when something you think will be good for the church doesn't come out of a drive to build your own kingdom, and the church doesn't go along with the idea, you may just end up with a grateful heart that you didn't take off in that direction. You just may develop a little more love that you were helped to see what they already know or could see and kept you from a lot of work only to lead to discouragement. While I was pastor in DeKalb, I used the deacons as a sounding board. If I had an idea I would go to them first, and they were always gracious to listen and give me honest feedback. If it was something they knew, from years and years of living in the community and being in that church, it wouldn't fly, they would tell me. And in many cases they would tell me why. Either it had been done before and didn't work, or there was a good reason it wouldn't work. I appreciated that, and since I didn't have a chip on my shoulder coming from a personal agenda of my own making, my feelings weren't hurt over it. Not having a personal agenda can save you from a lot of heartache and headache. John 3:30, let the pride be removed, grow in surrender and humility. Remember, God honors that.

I hope you understand from what you just read that I am getting at the idea of being a servant—a servant leader like Jesus was. Too many times we hear the nightmare stories from former church members that the pastor was a "my way or the highway" kind of pastor. That is not what you are called to. You are called to love God's people—not your people, God's people. You are called to love the lost, and you can't do that if you have a personal agenda where people need to be serving you and doing whatever you instruct them to do so you can brag about things at the next convention among your pastor buddies or in an attempt to build your resume for when that next bigger church calls and wants to talk to you.

It's the difference between having a personal agenda and kingdom agenda. And I am not over spiritualizing anything with that comment—that is just a genuine truth. Whose kingdom are you seeking to build? It's one or the other. If it is about you, trust me, take the lessons of history that kingdom will fall. If you are set on helping to build the kingdom of God then you will do things for His glory, not your own, things to make Jesus increase in every way, not you, and the work you do in that effort will make an eternal impact.

Chapter 6

GRACE FOLLOWS GRACE

This bit of advice is somewhat of a wrap-up thought. The idea first began with a comment from a dear friend in the ministry when I was in Texarkana, Rodney Thomas. Interesting story on how we became friends. I won't go into the details completely. The short version is that not long after I became the pastor at Highland Park, I received a phone call, and the voice on the other end just said, "You and I have a mutual friend." He then went on to say that mutual friend was Brother Billy Crosby. Well at that point whoever this person was, I was in! Rodney went on to explain that he had been Brother Billy's youth minster a number of years ago. It began to come back to me—Rodney had come to Northwest Memorial to preach a youth revival when I was in high school. I remembered him.

Interesting side note, Wayne Watson led the music for that Youth Revival. Anyway, Rodney had been in ministry, pastoring, and his parents owned a business in Texarkana. When his father became ill, he moved back home to help with the business. I began going to visit Rodney on a somewhat regular basis. I don't remember the situation, but in one of those counseling sessions Rodney made the comment, "If you are going to err, always err to the side of grace." I've never forgotten that, and out of it comes this bit of advice: grace follows grace.

Think about it for a moment. Whatever the situation may be, a positive one or a difficult one, grace follows grace. So, a few situations to see this.

There was a time when I had to dismiss, fire, a staff member, and it wasn't pretty. I tried the best I could to be gracious though it was a difficult set of circumstances, and the person involved was not happy about it or wanting to cooperate. I even tried helping the person understand this bit of advice. "Listen," I said, "if you will leave with grace, then I am certain grace will come after you." This person wasn't willing to, and when it came time for the deacons and personnel committee to consider a severance package, well, there wasn't much to it. When this person, who had been out of town a few days, came back and asked for a few extra days to move their things out, there wasn't much grace given to extend that. And I will add I had nothing to do with those decisions, nor did I try to influence the decisions. Consequently, the next place this person went to serve didn't last long either.

On the other side of it, dealing with me. After the situation had settled down, I was approached by several of our deacons, who told me if anything like this ever needed to happen again, they wanted to take care of it for me so I wouldn't have to. Grace was following grace.

In each church I have left, and only two of those were they difficult situations in which I left under duress, I did my best to leave with grace regardless of how I was treated. I can honestly tell you that the Lord brought grace to us through each one. That shows up in any number of ways. In some it was when people of the church would come by and visit before we left and tell us how sorry they were we were leaving and in some cases even give us money to help with the move. Other times they would tell us they knew the truth of what happened and were sorry for how it came about. We were loved, and that was a form of grace that encouraged us.

When we made a move feeling the Lord was leading and the situation was good, we still did what we could to leave with grace. And the Lord blessed those as well. We still have good relationships with people in those churches, and in the new places there was always a measure of God's grace that one way or another showed up better than before.

I believe this is something to teach your church. Whether it is a staff member or church member who leaves, be gracious to that person as he or she leaves and God will bring grace on the church in return. Even if it is a situation where the staff person did wrong and needed to be fired, there is still a way to do so with grace to that person. God honors that in a church.

After all, isn't it the grace of God that brings salvation? And then the grace of God that helps us through life.

I love Evangelist Bill Stafford! Brother Billy Crosby would have him come to our church every year for revival services. I have been to see Brother Bill preach in several different locations as I was able to through the years. In the column of my Bible I have a note from one of Brother Bill's sermons. It is in 2 Corinthians 12:7–10, Paul's thorn in the flesh and prayer and statement about strength in weakness that comes from God. The note is dated January 16, 2000, actually two different notes. Above verse 7 I have written, "Difficulty is the doorway to discovery." And then alongside verses 8–10 I wrote, "For every difficulty there is a river of grace." Both of these were comments that Brother Bill Stafford made in a sermon.

God's grace—it saves us and then it grows us. Let it work that way not only in you but through you to others in how you treat them. Regardless of the situation, do all that you can to make sure for your part there is grace. I am convinced by personal experience that God will cause grace to follow after you.

Some Closing Thoughts

The privilege of being called "pastor" is one of the greatest in life. You will have the opportunity to experience things no one else will. For example, I have been in the hospital by the bedside of a dying church member with their family as they say good-bye, only to leave that room and go to another floor as a young family welcomes their first child. I have had the thrill of being the first person called when a church member shoots their first deer, wanting me to come see it.

One November day I stood alongside a family as they watched their livelihood, a dairy farm, being loaded onto cattle trailers and sold off after years of losing money. Only then less than a year later I stood with the same family in their brand new chicken houses as the first load of little chicks were delivered, a baby chick in both hands, and asked to pray that God will bless the business as well as give Him praise for His provision. On two occasions I was able to stand with a family as they watched their home go up in flames. And then many times I would have a baby dedication service and then years later baptize that same child as he or she came to the place of inviting Jesus into his or her heart.

Yes, there are things I miss about being the pastor of a local church. So I want to encourage you as you begin to *Start Strong*. I offer this advice for your consideration and pray that you will experience the power of the presence of God in every setting you find yourself during the ministry. Don't go at it alone! Seek to build relationships with other pastors in your area. If you are Southern Baptist, get involved in your local association, get to know your director of missions, spend time with others. It is a blessed calling. My prayer is that God will reveal Himself to you constantly and show you His glory!

Appendix

From Pastor to Associational Director of Missions

I mentioned in chapter 3 that I would include the story on how or why I left the pastorate to become a director of missions. It is possible that during your life God will lead you in different directions all within the realm of serving Him. That is what happened with me. To be honest, when I arrived in Bonham in 1993, I was the happiest guy on earth. I was married, had three great kids and a chocolate Labrador we named King, and was pastor of a church! What could be better? Nothing I thought.

In 1995 our director of missions retired. For some of you who may not be Southern Baptist, or even some of you who are but not connected in understanding the conventions and associations, here's a summary. In Southern Baptist life we have our national convention, and then each state has a convention and the states are then set up with many associations. Typically, across Texas these are geographically set up by individual counties. The more west and south you travel in Texas the more sparsely the population becomes and so associations may cover several counties, but in East Texas and North Central Texas it is a county set-up. Bonham is located in Fannin County, and so our association was the Fannin Baptist Association. The director of missions serves as a consultant to the churches of the association. He has no authority over any church but is there to encourage and resource churches in any way he can. When our director of missions, Morris Robbins, retired, I was asked to serve on the search committee to find a new person.

At the time I did not know much about what this person's role was among our churches, and so I listened to what the other pastors on the committee had to say. I cannot find in any of my personal journals the specific day, but because of what I recorded for one meeting, I believe it possibly to have been January 24, 1995, but I will never forget that day nonetheless. There were four other pastors on the committee, each of them older than I was and with many more years of experience. We were sitting in the associational office discussing what kind of person we wanted to look for. These men began to talk about finding a man who would be a pastor to the pastors, who would meet with us at our weekly lunch and prayer meetings, who would come by our churches to see how we were doing and would essentially be an encourager. I will never forget the thoughts and feelings I began to have. To me they were describing the perfect ministry position. I still remember thinking to myself in those moments that if I had one or two more years of pastoral experience, I would have asked to be removed from the committee because I wanted to put name in for consideration of the position. I go back to that day now over twenty years later knowing that was the moment the desire and even calling to be a director of missions began for me. I continued to pastor and stay very involved in associational work in each of the pastorates I held.

Off and on for years the thought of becoming an associational director of missions returned. On more than one occasion now being in Bowie County and so the Bowie Baptist Association, while at First Baptist Church DeKalb, pastors would call me for information and advice on things. On one occasion during our summer children's camp where I was the director, a member of one of the churches in the area was talking with me about some things, and out of the blue he asked, "Why can't you be our director of missions?" One slightly awkward moment came when I was going with our senior adults to an event and our chairman of deacons was driving the van. I was in the passenger seat and we were talking about different things, and the topic of one of the church's previous pastors came up who is now a director of missions. Bobby (the chairman of deacons) asked me just what a director of missions did and I explained it to him. He then said, "That sounds like something you would be good at. Is that something you would be interested in?" For a moment, I wondered how I should answer my chairman of deacons on this.

I loved when pastors would call me about associational things and some even regarding state convention information. More and more this old desire began to grow, and these comments and questions from pastors seemed to be giving confirmation on a ministry change.

I attended a conference in 2009 put on by the North American Mission Board of the Southern Baptist Convention for New and Potential Directors of Missions. The conference confirmed for me that this was the next ministry step that I would take. Following the conference, I began sending my resume to associations who were in the process of seeking a new director of missions.

Three years would pass before I was contacted by the Guadalupe Baptist Association with their office in Victoria, Texas. The process went well, and I accepted the call to become their next director. I announced to First Baptist Church in April that I would be leaving after serving them for eleven years, and I began this new ministry on June 1, 2012.

Becoming a director of missions was a change that I thought I was prepared for but was more of a change than I anticipated. For a little more than twenty years my life schedule consisted of studying and writing to prepare three new sermons every week. Now I found myself with time on my hands that I had not had before, and it was a difficult adjustment. There were some things that I found very enjoyable. About two weeks on the field I remember sitting in my office and suddenly noticing how relaxed I was.

It dawned on me that the pressure of writing three sermons a week had taken more of a toll than I had known. I will admit I do not miss monthly deacon meetings or church business meetings, and I often share in churches where I may be preaching for the first time describing to them who I am to and for them that I work for and with fifty-four churches and that I have authority in none of them. I am enjoying that.

So, the Lord put a spark in my heart to be a pastor to pastors and encourager of churches. That's how it began. I still have a heart for pastors. You guys are the heroes of the faith. I want to cheer you on and encourage you every way I can. Again, it is my prayer that these six chapters of advice will help you start strong and stay strong. You can do it, for we have a mighty God who has brought you to where you are and will not leave you alone.

Printed in the United States
By Bookmasters